CHARLIE BLACK

by Malcolm Black

Published by Threepeppers Publishing

Copyright © 2021 Malcolm Black, pseudonym
Copyright © 2021 Threepeppers Publishing

Malcolm Black has asserted her right under the Copyright, Designs and Patents Act, 1988, to be identified as the author of this work.

All rights reserved. No part of this book shall be reproduced, stored in a retrieval system, or transmitted by any means – electronic, mechanical, photocopying, recording, or otherwise – without written permission from the author and the publisher.

1st Edition – May 2021

ISBN: 9781838494308

Cover:
Memories of Hope
Photo Collage © Malcolm Black

www.3peppers.co.uk

To my son

Foreword

One day, Charlie may write his own story, or possibly he may not. I cannot write his story, because it will only be through the fullness of time that he will come to terms with the experience, what he thought, what he felt and how he pulled himself along his road to recovery.

This story is unashamedly mine, his father, divorced parent to two teenagers who live with me. Like every father and son, we have had our ups and downs. At times it has not only been far from perfect; it has been positively awful on a day-to-day basis. But during the months prior to the accident, we had become close. Covid-19 lockdown in the spring of 2020 gave an opportunity to stop life as we know it, to remove ourselves from the pressures and challenges that our busy lives cause, and for me to once again enjoy the role of being a parent.

When lockdown ended and schools reopened, some of those pressures resurfaced, but beneath it all there remained a stronger bond than before. The advent of a new partner in my life had caused some challenge. It is difficult when you feel dad has only been there for you and now there is somebody else taking a lot of his time and affection. And the return to school had provoked some difficult scenarios. School experience had never been a resounding success for Charlie and some elements were becoming increasingly difficult with the expectations the system places on children, especially those with a diagnosis of ADHD. But that bond between father and son had not been broken and my approach of fighting fire with water was increasingly making conflict shorter and less intense when it occurred. Every phone call, every parting, every day always ended with the same sentences initiated by one of other of us: "Love you, Son", "Love you, Dad".

I've not used my son's real name in this book, primarily because he is quite a private child and I do not want him to be 'the kid that book was written about'.

So why 'Charlie Black'?

When a child first goes into ICU at King's College Hospital, before full details are taken from parents, the child is assigned a first name from the phonetic alphabet and a second name of a colour. It was just a couple of days in when I noticed the name 'Charlie Black' still on a sheet above my son's bed. It seemed like such a good name, and thus, for a brief while, he became known as 'Charlie Black'. Three months later, the name is now the seed of an idea, to form an organisation working with children recovering from brain injuries, providing a service to rural areas and enabling them to take part in creative and therapeutic activities – Charlie Black CIC (Community Interest Company).

And that is one of the essential elements of the healing journey. Through such a deeply traumatic event, there has to be a way to ensure that good triumphs over negativity. Challenge can bring out the best of us and in Charlie's case he surprised the most seasoned medical staff with the speed, determination and success of his journey to recovery.

Some events of his life stand out in their own right. One in particular, when he had just turned eight, showed his care and determination not to give up; it is a determination that I believe I would later witness as he lay in that hospital bed fighting for his life. In his first Junior Sports Day, as the line of boys started the 200M race, one of his friends stumbled and fell. As the rest ran off, Charlie stopped, picked up his friend, checked a teacher was coming and then restarted running. He could have stopped. He could have given up. But he chose to run, way behind all the other racers, in spite of the embarrassment that was clear to see even at a distance. As he came down the home strait, the entire school and assembled parents, all of whom had seen his act of kindness, rose to their feet to applaud and cheer him on. In those few moments, Charlie showed us the very best of the lad that would one day need that single-minded determination to push aside expectations and simply run the race by himself. It gave me one of my proudest moments ever in his life, up until that fateful, life-changing night.

This book also records the tumultuous rollercoaster of emotions that fill your mind as you watch your precious child literally fight for their life. Above all, it is a journey of hope, for Charlie has surpassed the expectations of the amazing team that worked with him. Looking at his MRI, we have been told on more than one occasion that he simply should not be able to do what he is doing. He is our miracle. This is his moment, the moment when he did more than we all thought he ever could. And this story is my journey alongside my son in his darkest hour.

During the long hours of silence, sitting beside his bed or on the endless train journeys back and forth from home to hospital, I kept a record of his progress. I knew that without it, I would forget so many details, so many moments of fear, of heartache and of extraordinary joy. In spite of the pain that so much of this journey causes, I do not ever want to forget that in its own way it has also been beautiful.

This book is also dedicated to those extraordinary people who were there through the most traumatic, yet also most magnificent moments that we experienced. The First Responders from Tesco who were by his side immediately to give assistance within moments of the accident; the paramedics and Air Ambulance Crew whose training and skill made the difference between life and death. The medical staff, that team of the most astonishing people, who showed unbelievable care not just for Charlie but for all of us throughout his time in hospital. It is impossible to overstate the impact that those wonderful people have had on our lives and the sense of gratitude and respect that we all hold for them. There are also those people who play a less obvious part in a hospital, but who still make a difference; the cleaners, those who bring the meals, and the lovely staff at Costa Coffee with whom I formed a bond and who, in some of the dark moments, just gave a smile and a warm, encouraging comment that lifted my spirits.

What follows are the posts written at the time, which serve as the framework for this book. Alongside those blogs, I've added more narrative of the journey that has taken place and that will continue for many months to come.

This book and the company named after his ICU identity are both a tribute to my son – truly my hero!

Note from the Publisher

The chapters of this book include sections printed in italic. These are the original blog entries as written by the author and left untouched in the original format, including the emoticons and emojis used.

1 - Trauma

"THAT'S MY SON!"

Three words that I have used in different contexts but each time with extreme emotion since that moment at approximately 7:15 p.m. on Halloween night 2020. They were shouted with pure fear as the paramedic held up her hand to stop my car unaware of who I was, and as I ran to him lying in the gutter, my simple anxiety turned into a primeval, gut-wrenching pain that consumed every single part of my being. There lay my son, in my arms, eyes heavily dilated, face badly smashed up, moaning gently in pain with blood coming from his nose and vomiting. It's a pain that a parent never wants to feel and even as I write this, three months after the event, the tears are flowing readily at the thought of that scene, the pain once again fills my body and the full awfulness of the sight that greeted me hits me hard.

Half an hour earlier I'd just arrived at my partner's house, ready to relax with a meal knowing that my daughter was enjoying the company of her old primary school friends nearby and Charlie had phoned me earlier to say he was heading out with his mates. Then came the life-changing moment that, even as I took the call, didn't yet strike me as having the impact it ultimately would. My ex-wife phoned to say she'd had a call from a friend who had picked up his phone, that he'd been hit by a car and was unconscious. The need for speed to get to him and a deep anguish as to how badly he'd been hurt consumed me.

I rang my daughter, managed to drive round to where she was, grabbed her and made a 15-minute journey in just 7 minutes. I came to a halt with the sight of police cars and an ambulance all beside a body lying in the road. I stopped the engine, leapt out, didn't even bother to close the door. The paramedic was holding her hand up to stop me but the moment I yelled out those three words she let me come close.

And there he lay.

My mind became confused. I spoke to him, trying to reassure him, telling him it would be okay. And then his head turned, he vomited and blood started coming from his nose. A searing, panicked pain took over every part of me. For those few moments, I knew how close I was to losing him.

And yet surreal thoughts still filled my head. I believed that at any moment he'd suddenly come to, shake his head, I'd take him home and a couple of paracetamols later he'd be fine. A helicopter was overhead; the Air Ambulance. I looked up and wondered who it was there for. Surely not my child? Surely, he wasn't hurt that bad?

The paramedic told me just to keep holding him and keep talking as they got him on to a stretcher and transferred him to the ambulance. He was still unresponsive, but moaning gently. They began performing the tests that I've seen so many times on television reality programmes of which I'm a devotee. Yet all of a sudden it was me standing there looking at my precious child, and with every single second that passed, I desperately hoped and prayed that he wouldn't go downhill.

The Air Ambulance crew arrived. They were astonishing and instantly through my pain I felt a sense of reassurance. But then came the harsh reality. Charlie was clearly displaying signs of a bleed on the brain. They were going to intubate and place him into an induced coma. This was way beyond what I had imagined when I took the call and at that moment the full gravity of life never being the same again hit me hard.

Charlie's mum arrived on the scene with her partner. We agreed that she'd go in the helicopter – a slight relief as I'd said I would go before she arrived but I'm terrified of flying. The last thing I wanted to do was distract the crew through my own inability to travel in the air without nausea. My daughter and I would travel under blues and twos in a police car and my ex-wife's partner would follow us up to ensure we'd got transport home.

I kissed Charlie on the forehead, painfully and honestly wondering if I would see him alive again and just praying that a miracle would occur.

The journey was a blur. Overwhelming. Anxiety once again consumed every part of me. The tears barely stopped rolling down my cheeks. I did my best to comfort his sister with my words and to check she was okay. She'd also witnessed the sight of him lying in the gutter at his most fragile and vulnerable and I knew that with every deep emotion I was experiencing, she'd be mirroring them all in the torturous journey alongside me.

With speeds far in excess of anything I could have managed under my own steam, we reached the front of King's College Hospital just as the Air Ambulance was arriving. I looked up and there he was arriving in the sky above me. I stood, frozen on the spot. Odd thoughts still filled my mind. should I film this moment? Because surely he'd be awake in a couple of hours, we would be chatting happily, and he would want to see the moment for himself. Yet it also seemed deeply inappropriate to think of something so trivial when I had no idea of how he was doing, or even, at that moment, if he was still alive. I had no idea whether he'd ever be able to respond, to understand, to communicate, to express his feelings.

And then there was the waiting.

With the inevitable silence in the waiting room, I logged on to social media and saw questions from those within my community. It was at that time I knew that I would need to record this journey, partly as my method for coping, but also for Charlie to understand what he'd been through, what we'd all been through, and how difficult this journey may be….

Saturday 31st October – 11 p.m.

Everybody I know who has a faith, please say a prayer for Charlie. I've just arrived at King's courtesy of the police as the air ambulance has landed with Charlie on board. He's been knocked over and has head injuries. Awaiting news. 🙏🙏🙏🙏🙏🙏🙏🙏

Update: Charlie is currently in an induced coma whilst they assess the bleed on his brain. He has some broken bones in his face, shoulder and pelvis. So right now, it's a waiting game.

The sense of helplessness with my child's life in the hands of others and an inability to enter the department due to Covid-19 restrictions was overwhelming. In any other circumstance, I'd have been there beside him, able to hold his hand, able to offer words of comfort from a familiar voice, able to see for myself how he was doing. But in this cruel pandemic, just like so many others, there was no access. And I didn't know what else to do other than seek to support of others through their prayers, love and positive thoughts. A screen felt like a safe and familiar place. And I knew others would instantly respond, supporting all of us from the earliest part of this journey, lifting us up, holding us. I felt the impact almost immediately.

In the early hours, Charlie was transferred from A&E on to ICU and, for the first time since he'd left the scene of the accident, I was able to see and touch my son.

He looked dreadful. He had tubes and sensors all over him. His right eye was completely closed; black, blue and swollen. His left eye was fractionally open, but heavily dilated under the sedation of the coma. His face and head were red raw from the double impact his head had received: firstly from the now heavily dented bonnet of the Jeep, and secondly when his head hit the road as he landed. A machine beside him was breathing for him. And he was completely motionless.

It was then that the rollercoaster of emotions kicked in for the first time. A deep traumatic distress was tempered by a sense of relief and joy that he was at least alive. That joy was tempered by the deep anxiety of how much of him would ever return – would this be Charlie from now on? Would he ever truly experience the joy of running freely, laughing and joking?

I kissed him gently on his wounded forehead. I whispered into his ear words of encouragement, words of love, words that I hoped he would hear deep within his lost consciousness, words that I hoped would help him as he battled for his life.

Around 3 a.m. I travelled home. The journey was a silent, exhausted one. The sense of emptiness pervaded my being. I couldn't find thoughts and words that would connect in any logical way. I was consumed with endless guilt. Why wasn't I there to protect him? Yet I knew there was no way I could have followed my teenage son around.

On arrival home I went upstairs into his bedroom. It was, as always, a complete mess. I knelt down and I sobbed, uncontrollably. From deep within my soul, I howled like an animal, an intensity of pain that couldn't be expressed in any other way. And I begged God and the Universe to protect my son, to keep him alive, to watch over him in his darkest hour.

I went to my bed and the sheer exhaustion of the entire, dreadful experience forced my body into a deep but disturbed sleep.

2 – Finding the light in the tunnel

Sunday 1st November

Firstly, from all of us - thank you. We've been strengthened, supported and uplifted by the care and love shown towards us.

Charlie's friends who were there were brilliant. They showed care and initiative. They got us there to support him. They made a difference and created a positive narrative about teenagers.

Charlie is still in an induced coma. This evening they have succeeded in getting a meds drip in, which is good. The ophthalmic consultant has examined his eye and in spite of a bone fracture, the function of the eye appears unaffected.

We have been passing on all your messages. I know he can hear them. He is calm, his cranial pulse is nice and low and the bleed on the brain seems to be receding. They have managed to drain his lung pretty well and it looks quite good.

I sense he's fighting. Your love, prayers and support are tremendously uplifting for us all.

Thank you so much.

I have tried to respond to as many messages as I can individually, but forgive me if I have missed anybody.

I will update you with progress tomorrow.

Thank you XXXX

I can't begin to express the impact of the love, care and support that flew through the internet throughout those first hours. Many people are private, and in their times of distress wish to share little or nothing of what's happening. Likewise, I had to weigh up the issues of privacy for Charlie – but so many of his friends, relatives and people who had seen or heard of the accident were already desperate to know how he was and how serious things were. In those darkest times, no matter how many people are there beside you in the ward, you haven't yet had the opportunity to form the relationships with them and it's all in an unfamiliar place. The messages that flowed back and forth punctuated the long silent times of waiting; they formed a crucial link between the reality that I knew and this surreal, frightening place. And writing messages and the blogs helped me hold it all together – I had to string cohesive sentences and phrases that kept those we know and love informed. It enabled a clarity of focus to my mind that simply staring at the walls, tubes and my poor smashed up child wouldn't have achieved.

With every message that pinged on to my phone, there was a tangible sense of the love, the positive thoughts, prayers and good wishes of all those I knew as well as many I'd never met. Likewise, the blogs had an almost immediate impact on the social media network in our home locality. We can all too easily become immersed in tales of bad parking and dog poo, but Charlie was known by so many people in our neighbourhood. His plight instantly brought a community together and gave a common focus on something that really mattered to the lovely people following the story. Even in those first few hours, it was clear that Charlie was having an impact and that his personality would affect hundreds of people in a positive way.

At this stage, the medical issues were paramount. Thoughts of long-term rehabilitation were a million miles away from simply hoping and praying that the bleed on his brain would heal, and give hope to a sense of recovery. Every word I spoke was aimed at either encouraging him to fight or telling him what was happening so that in the event of an awakening he'd be calmer. He tells me he can't remember any of the things that I said at that time and that he simply felt like he was dreaming. But when he did finally awaken, there was no sense of panic, no asking where he was or why; he knew where he was and what had happened, even though he'd got no direct memory of the accident itself.

Monday 2nd November

Once again, from all of us, thank you so much for the love, care and prayers you have poured in our direction. I have spent much of my time beside Charlie reading out those beautiful messages. We are overwhelmed in the most wonderful way.

Today Charlie had a procedure to place filters in his arteries to prevent clots. That shows confidence in his strength. The procedure all went well. Tonight, he's had his first food, protein milk, fed through tube but it's food nonetheless.

If his night is stable, they are proposing to start the process of waking him tomorrow afternoon. This is both positive and terrifying. It's on waking that any neurological issues will be revealed. But our wish, of course, is to be able to talk with him, comfort him and share the love being shown to him by so many.

Thank you again for lifting us all up. Through the darkest of situations, you have shone light.

The light shone brightly.

But the paradoxical thought processes on the prospect of awakening were unbelievably challenging. On the plus side, we'd been told that it could be days, weeks or even months before they would feel confident he was stable enough to wake; yet here we were, just a couple of days after the accident and they were discussing waking him. On the negative side, we knew that the awakening was also going to reveal potential neurological damage and any physical incapacity resulting from the brain injury.

We also knew that with coming out of the coma, the physical injuries he sustained could result in awful pain. Whilst he was in the coma, he was protected from all of that; his body was still and peaceful and this highly active lad felt no frustration at his inability to move. We'd been told to prepare for confusion and distress. Whilst we'd been endlessly talking to him about where he was and what had happened, there was no guarantee that any of that would have been processed. It was a real possibility that he'd wake in a state of panic, unaware of what had happened, horrified by the tubes coming out of him everywhere and potentially unable to move parts of his body. And on first waking, he'd still have the tube in his throat which could cause a great deal of panic and he may struggle to breathe by himself initially.

Tuesday 3rd November a.m.

Good morning everybody.

It's difficult to articulate the range of emotions that we've all got as a family right now. But the knowledge that there are so many of you wishing to uphold us all on the journey we have found ourselves in has a profoundly uplifting effect. We are not alone.

From the bottom of our hearts, thank you.

In his own, inimitable way, Charlie is uniting people and bringing out the best in others. As awful and distressing as this whole experience is, it is also humbling and one that fills us with hope in humanity.

Thank you XXXX

I wrote this early in the morning with an intense sense of foreboding about what the day would bring, but an equally deep sense of the love and goodwill that surrounded us in what was about to happen over the following hours.

3 – The Awakening

Tuesday 3rd November p.m.

Thank you all again. In this awful dark tunnel, you are shining brightly. Charlie's plight is showing the very best of community, kindness and love and we all continue to feel wonderfully supported by your good wishes, prayers, positive energy and love.

They briefly woke Charlie a bit this afternoon to give an initial neurological test. He moved arms, hands and his right leg. The team believe his left leg was hindered by the pelvic fracture.

Once back within his coma, he was given a CT scan in which all looks okay. The cranial pulse bolt was then removed as the team felt confident to do so.

Charlie's slow, careful recovery journey continues to go according to plan. So tomorrow they will begin the process of a more permanent awakening.

It's at that stage any neurological issues will begin to surface.

Thank you all again. We feel extraordinarily privileged to have such a supportive network xx

---

I knew before what tear ducts were all about, but I never realised just how much they could work in such a short period of time. It was the sight of those first movements that triggered yet another waterfall from my eyes; the sense that somewhere deep within that brain temporarily locked away, Charlie was still there and responding to some of the instructions given to him by the team.

We had just a few minutes to talk to him before he was placed once again in the coma, just a few precious minutes to tell him how much we loved him, to give him words of encouragement to keep him fighting, to tell him that no matter what, we'd be there for him and that everything was going to be okay. And then he was once again placed into the coma to protect his brain from too much activity whilst he was taken for his scan.

The process of moving him was an extraordinary display of choreographed care in every single movement. Each person had their assigned role, with every step being taken so carefully so as not to raise the brain activity. Each time the monitor on his brain reached a level of 20, the entire process was halted to allow him to calm down. Each part of the journey was clearly articulated and the route cleared of obstacles. It was an insight not only into the astonishing professionalism of the team, but into the extraordinary level of care he was receiving in every part of this journey. One nurse was in charge. With each instruction, the others simply listened and followed. Nobody took offence. Nobody expressed disagreement. Nobody dissented. It was all about Charlie and in its own way was a beautiful process to observe, filling me with such an enormous confidence that there was no finer place in the world, no better level of care and expertise than that which he was receiving right now.

Equally heart-warming was the removal of the cranial pulse bolt upon his return, a vital piece of kit that had been inserted through a hole drilled into his skull and that showed his brain had settled enough to be out of danger. This was hugely significant. I was told at a later stage that upon arrival, with the amount of damage to Charlie's brain, on a scale of 1 to 3 where 3 is the most dangerous, Charlie was a 3. Yet here we were, just three days later witnessing one of the many stages of miracle that we'd live through on this extraordinary journey.

Wednesday 4th November a.m.

I've just arrived. I said into his ear, "Charlie, it's Dad".

He lifted his arm right up beside his head.

It's honestly one of the most beautiful things I could ever have seen.

It is impossible to describe moments like this, but the surge of emotion was similar to the moment of his birth. And there are many parallels. The waiting may have been much shorter between accident and awakening than the nine long months of pregnancy, but the sense of joy, relief, exhilaration, exhaustion and foreboding were all as powerful as they had been fourteen-and-a-half years earlier when he first greeted the world. It was the sense of recognition that was the most powerful; he knew it was me, that I was there right beside him, comforting him, caring for him, helping to clean him, tending to his every need, protecting him. I needed to know he'd felt those things every bit as much as he'd needed to hear it.

His acknowledgement of my greeting was the first moment where I had a sense that things were going to be all right. We didn't yet have any clear indication of how much he would be able to do, but there was communication and for the first time the knowledge that he knew I was there, that he knew he wasn't alone. However much or little, the ability to communicate and receive a response secured the relationship. I knew he could hear my words and that in some way I'd be able to bring him comfort, understanding and that he'd know how much I loved him and would be there for him through this perilous experience.

Wednesday 4th November p.m.

Here we go. Waking process beginning 🙏 🙏🙏🙏🙏🙏

Wednesday 4th November evening

We continue to see positive signs in Charlie's recovery. Today they have brought him out of the coma and removed his breathing tube. He is now breathing for himself and still unconscious but comfortable. The team seemed happy with how things went today and are not unduly worried that he hasn't fully woken - it can take several days. At least he is not distressed and his body is healing whilst he sleeps.

Over the next few days, we will learn of any issues in his neurological function, but when he first came out of the coma, he squeezed hands and wiggled toes when asked, so there are positive signs.

With each day that passes, we all continue to feel supported by the tsunami of kindness and support from so many people, a number of whom we have never even met. In this emotional rollercoaster, your support is giving us a solid foundation. Thank you.

The team at King's are astonishing. We are so grateful that he's being cared for by the finest team in the world.

Over the next few days there will probably be fewer significant steps to tell you of, but please uphold Charlie in your thoughts, prayers and positive vibes as he re-joins the world.

Thank you XX

I knew at the time that this blog somewhat sugar-coated the process of the awakening, but I was so very determined to share just the good news of this miraculous process. The reality of watching your child go through the extrication of the breathing tube is, quite simply, distressing. Charlie's discomfort was obvious. He choked, he reached, he coughed and spluttered. His face pulled expression for the first time since the accident – not of relief but of distress. As the tube came out the team sucked excess saliva to clear his airways. And then, as they manually pumped air in, his brain had to remind him how to breathe all over again. Failure to do so would result in a second intubation, which I'd already been warned wouldn't be pleasant and was likely to be distressing for Charlie.

Then, once more, he coughed, spluttered and started to breathe for himself. The regular experience of a wave of relief washed over me. Just four days in and his beautiful face was free of the breathing tube; my child was beginning to resemble the one before the accident and whilst there would be many tense moments as he re-learned the art of breathing and clearing excess saliva from his throat, he had succeeded in one more significant step in his journey. His eyes were opened more, but it was almost impossible to work out what was going on behind them. They were unnervingly vacant, hollow, expressionless. Yet we still had little signs that something was going on inside his locked brain and that before long we'd get more positive clues that things would be okay. With every single, passing hour, my son was showing me a resilience and determination that took my breath away and that filled me with hope and pride.

Thursday 5th November

Wow! This is intense today!

This evening Charlie has been moved from ICU to HDU. That's good. It means they're confident that things are improving consistently. We've been fortunate that they let his sister spend some time with him today as well as his mother and me.

He's had his eyes open several times in the last half hour and has focused on my face as I've talked to him. He's quite fidgety, but that's showing us that physically he's in much better shape than they initially believed.

Each little step of progress gives us a euphoric boost and the sense of overwhelming primeval pain that we initially felt is being replaced by optimism with each new achievement.

As with every other day, your love, care, prayers and thoughts are upholding us through this most difficult of times.

Thank you 🙏❤️😊 XX

This was the first day when some of the deep anxiety started to recede. Charlie had been breathing for himself for a full 24 hours without drama. And his body movements showed a much greater level of mobility than I'd expected to witness. Where I'd been told of the multiple fractures to face, shoulders and pelvis, I'd expected to see both immobility and pain. Instead, I'd seen a great deal of fidgeting! So much so that special padding was required on each side of his bed to prevent him from harming himself on the hard bedframe.

The move to HDU also meant that I was now able to camp beside his bed each night. It lacked comfort, it lacked privacy, it totally lacked peace and tranquillity. But it also meant that when he fully woke, there would be somebody beside him no matter what time of the day or night. So, for the next few weeks life took on a new routine. Each day there would be a break when his mother would take over, enabling me to head back to Kent, have a shower, change clothes, endeavour to prepare some sort of meal for his sister, briefly see to the dogs, throw washing in the machine, hoover and then head back to London for the night. Sometimes it would be two nights on the trot, with just a cramped shower/toilet room with a shower head that kept falling off, but one in which I could get myself a little presentable and smell slightly better for the new day!

There's no doubting the exhaustive nature of such a routine, but in its own way it was also extraordinarily comforting. It was safe. It became familiar. I knew Charlie was in the best hands so there was no need to fear for his wellbeing.

Much as the familiarity of the routine quickly brought some stability to my existence, my disconnection with the rest of the world also became prevalent in my activity. Once in the hospital, that disconnection didn't really matter, but outside, life was carrying on oblivious to the trauma surrounding Charlie. In my more relaxed frame of mind, I found small moments where the emotion started to flow through in the least likely of places. A small memory, an image, a message from somebody; all these would unexpectedly overwhelm me causing the tears once more to flow. Thankfully the slight tint in my glasses and the necessitous wearing of facemasks due to Covid-19 meant that much of that was hidden. But every time I had to message somebody who was still unaware of what had happened, or I had to write and update, I was struck by the enormity of what was going on.

Months later, some words still hit me hard. When telling others of his story, it's the sharing of just how close he was to death that still hits me and even now in writing these words, the phrase "I nearly lost him" causes me to well up with emotion. Every parent I've met has understood how deep the wound cuts and I can see tears in their eyes as I tell them. Yet I keep using the phrase because its repetition gives me such immense gratitude every single day. It reminds me of how fortunate we were and prevents me from taking anything for granted with Charlie.

Friday 6th November

Firstly, thank you so much to those of you who have so generously donated to the Just Giving fund. We hadn't even thought about money, but thankfully friends had. Spending extra and not earning soon becomes scary, but we now know we can be at Charlie's side and give him the support he'll need without worrying.

Charlie is continuing to give us hopeful signs. He has responded to each of us when we have expressed our love for him. He has looked intently at us through several conversations and squeezed our hands when we ask and, beautifully, on one occasion when I told him I loved him. He is fidgety at times - but that is showing us that he has good body movement. He is also managing peaceful rest.

The wonderful team here are happy with the way things are moving and we continue to draw strength from that. Likewise, your thoughts, care, love and prayers relentlessly support all of us.

The journey is tough and we've experienced extremes of emotion, but the rollercoaster is levelling a little as we move slowly forward on Charlie's healing journey.

As always - thank you XX

It may seem trivial to have been thinking of practicalities in the first couple of days, but alongside our worries about Charlie were the concerns about finance. I'm self-employed and earlier in the year, Covid lockdown had caused an absence of earnings and a draining of savings. I'd just reached a point where it seemed like the world of earnings would return, with work lined up for several customers, when Charlie's accident happened. The financial reality of living miles away and not earning loomed like a dark cloud over me. Train and taxi fares swallowed up £40 per day, in addition to which I had to eat and drink, which swallowed another £25 per day. Later on in the experience, the weekend leave for Charlie meant that I was spending around

£200 per week on fuel, London driving charges and parking fees, in addition to the midweek train journey.

Of course, none of it was trivial. I had no idea of how much therapy Charlie would need when, ultimately, he would leave the hospital and what possible alterations to the home might be required. I'd already shifted some items of furniture in the full expectation that he wouldn't be able to do the steep stairs in a building of c.1850. All of this would need funding alongside a high level of care from me that could prevent me earning. At this moment, in spite of all these thoughts, I knew that the only place for me to be was at Charlie's bedside, but the act of a friend in setting up a Just Giving page on our behalf made such a difference. With all that was going on, the ability to buy a coffee and not worry about the mounting cost of such decadent luxuries just eased the whole experience on a daily basis. The walk down three flights of stairs to Costa gave respite to the intensity and, at times, boredom when things were or weren't happening. Seeing the same faces in the café created a link with normality several times each day and conversations created a fleeting bond. Before long they were asking about Charlie, and when, ultimately, he joined me on the excursion, it was a cause of celebration.

Charlie update – Saturday 7th

I find writing the day helps me know where in the week I am.

This time last week I was kneeling in the road beside Charlie thinking I was about to lose him.

It's impossible to quantify the primeval sense of pain in a moment like that. Our worlds were turned upside down and have yet to find a solid foundation. At a time like this, the distance between despair and euphoria is short, but euphoria has the edge.

Today he is showing further signs of progress. He's not yet fully responsive by any means, but when the nurse was dressing him, she asked him to put his arm through the sleeve on his t-shirt and he did. He's also squeezed our hands a few times when we've been talking to him. So the progress which at times seems so desperately slow is still progress. And our anxiety is about wanting to know Charlie isn't enduring suffering inside his partially locked in world.

The words 'thank you' still seem hopelessly inadequate, but from all of us it's deeply heartfelt. We really feel astonishingly fortunate and uplifted by you all.

When a child is in infancy, you celebrate every little step of development. You look for the smallest signs of the first word, the first small steps, the first independent actions when a child performs a task by themselves. Charlie was still unable to communicate through spoken word, but the sight of him being able to follow an instruction and to start to perform simple tasks brought a surge of encouragement. His eyes still didn't convey any particular sense of emotion, and in order to know he was looking at me I had to move my position to within his line of sight. But once there, I sensed he was focused on the familiar face, that he knew it was me, that he could absorb the encouragement. Each brief interaction was accompanied by a desperate desire for some sort of response, recognition or sign of emotion. And each little response felt like he'd passed a huge milestone in his life, that he'd achieved something extraordinary – and in its own way, he had.

Of course, each small step brought a rush of desperation for another step, a bigger step, a more permanent step. But the one thing that was needed above all else was patience. Almost every conversation with medical staff was accompanied by a reminder that this was going to be a slow journey, but equally the conversations started to be accompanied by expressions of surprise at just how much Charlie was already able to do. It was just one week since his accident, yet we were repeatedly being told that his progress was both consistent and happening with greater rapidity than expected. Charlie had fought for his life, and won! He now began to show us the determination in his journey to recovery and slowly, and surely, all my fears and concerns began to be replaced with an extraordinary sense of pride.

Charlie update - Sunday 8th

So, as I start to write, the music on Charlie's playlist has fired up, "I'm Still Standing". This should be a family anthem!

Today has felt like a long one. For parents that have been in this place before, it must have been similar. All around life carries on at its usual frenetic speed; in this experience the hours pass with the only aim being the opportunity to see the smallest of steps occur.

In reality, there's little to report. But the little seems like a lot. After I had helped bathe him this morning, he put his arm through his sleeve on my request. He squeezed my hand when I asked. He held my arm tightly. He watched intently as his mum played video clips from previous holidays. He's mouthing like he's trying to speak. He's scratching his nose when it itches. All things we wouldn't normally even think about, but things that we now delight in and celebrate.

Again today, thank you so much to those of you who have donated to the Just Giving. It's going to be used entirely for getting us back and forth and then for adaptions and equipment Charlie will need. And it's lifted an enormous burden from our shoulders, as have the countless offers of practical help. As the days pass, your care, love, interest and support hold strong. We look forward to the day when Charlie can sit on the corner by Tesco and thank you all personally XX

Like most parents, as much as we love our children there are days when we would rather they spoke a little less! It was a standing joke that Charlie had started making little noises from the moment he was born and had rarely stopped for breath since. The silent Charlie was unnerving and unfamiliar, so the first signs of lip movement as he made direct eye contact provoked immense joy and a sense of encouragement. I was desperate to make out words from the movement on his lips, but the movements were accompanied by nothing more than a faint sound of air. Nonetheless, it was incredibly positive to sense that he was trying to communicate and that any time soon we might expect to have words and sentences.

Charlie update - Monday 9th

The peaks and troughs of emotion that inexorably invade every hour continue. Today we met the senior neurologist who is overseeing Charlie's care. We're looking at the possibility of Charlie taking one of just two places on the 3-month intensive rehabilitation programme, which seems positive as they wouldn't invest all those resources unless they felt it was worth it.

But with the discussion of that option comes a dawning reality. In an instant, our lives were turned upside down, none more so than Charlie's. And at this moment in time, we have no real idea as to whether our previous normality will ever return. But we do know that we'll do whatever it takes to help Charlie every step of the way, so whatever commitment is required, we'll take it on!

To balance the moments of challenge, there have also been the moments of elation.

One of today's magic moments came with the physios. They asked him to open his eyes and look at me, which he did. They then asked him to reach out and grab my hand. He looked me straight in the eye, reached out, grabbed my hand and squeezed. It was honestly like 4,000 volts of emotion shooting through every part of me. In that briefest of moments, we connected and I knew I'd reached into Charlie's world. Likewise, his mum smothered his face with kisses and it prompted a smile - the first we have seen since the accident. He's been watching things intently, clearly absorbing the visual stimulus.

So much as the progress seems so depressingly slow, there are still those moments that exhaust me through sheer joy.

As always, thank you. Your support is astonishing XXX

Mondays have rarely felt so good! Yes, there was the prospect of a long journey. But the conversation about a three-month programme was a huge step forward from earlier conversations about six to twelve months, and with it came a real sense that the team overseeing his care could see good reasons for investing in him, a justification for pumping resources into him and in the belief that it would provide a good return.

The real moment of pure joy came with that recognition of my presence. It's impossible to overstate the euphoria that washed over me at that moment. Charlie has always been such a talker, so the silence since the accident and the inability to communicate effectively had been a trial. Now I'd got a real sense that he wanted to reach me from inside his locked world, that he wanted to express his feelings, that our worlds were connecting properly and that my limitless sense of hope was receiving positive affirmation through those small moments.

Charlie's Journey - Tuesday 10th

It's late into the evening and the ward is all at peace, including Charlie. Today It's really felt like he's preparing to return from his world back into ours. He's showing alert responses to a variety of stimulus. He really seemed like he wanted to join in with a conversation between his mum and nurses. He watched the film Avatar intently. His eyes are more focused, more vibrant as they search to make sense of what is going on. His look straight into our eyes reaches right in to us as he seeks to communicate from within his current world

For me, the most poignant burst of emotion came as the occupational therapists worked with him. He was sitting up, largely holding himself up. They asked him to reach for me and he leant in for a hug, snuggling in to my shoulder. The Occupational Therapist said she could see the expression of pleasure as he snuggled. It's in those moments that you most realise the strength of the bond between parent and child.

I'm aware that my updates are chronicling more of a journey between parent and child rather than just a medical report on Charlie. Forgive my indulgence, but it's partly because my coping mechanism is to write and partly because I want Charlie to have a record of how it felt as well as how he healed. There are others who are intensely engaged in his recovery and who will, of course, share their story with him too in the fulness of time.

Thank you for your continued support, love, prayers and comments. I know many of you are on this journey with him - deep down he'll know XX

Almost...almost...almost!!!

I could feel him trying to burst through with every interaction. The moment of the hug was one of many in which a wave of emotion washed over my soul. His head was turned away from me as he nestled into my shoulder, but the reaction of the

Occupational Therapist was clear: "Oh, I can see the comfort in his expression!"

It was the first time I knew Charlie recognised all the words, hugs, kisses and love were making a difference to him. When your child is a baby, you can swiftly receive the message that your efforts to comfort them are working. They fall over and cry, and a warm hug and loving words can soon stop the tears. They sense the reassurance you're offering and swiftly react to the reassurance you give, that it's going to be all right. In Charlie's locked world, I had no real knowledge of how much my words and actions were bringing him comfort and his expressionless face had given little away up to this point, so the knowledge that he'd shown a response, that he felt comforted, meant the world to me.

We've always hugged. We've always articulated the bond between father and son. So that moment, when he finally began to get some greater control over his movement, and give a very deliberate hug, was immense.

4 – The Return

Charlie's Journey - 11/11 morning

HE'S TALKING!
HE'S BACK WITH US!
HAPPY TEARS!!!!

Charlie's Journey – 11/11 evening

I'm inundated with messages! I'll try to answer them all over the next few hours.

Circumstances are doing their best to prevent me from feeling the sheer delight of the day. I drove to Tonbridge Station late due to his sister's birthday and on arrival discovered I'd got his mum's car keys in my pocket. I drove back. I returned. At the time of writing, I'm on the station platform reading the sign that tells me the train is cancelled, so I must wait. But I feel no sense of frustration.

This morning Charlie took us by surprise. His mum was with him (only 1 parent allowed at a time) and when the doctor said "Hi!", Charlie looked at him and replied, "Hi". When the doctor asked if he was okay, he replied, "Yeah".

His mum grabbed the phone, facetimed his sister and Charlie's first full sentence since waking was, "Happy birthday Eleanor. I love you!"

The nurse called me in, and his mum asked what he wanted to say to me. He looked me straight in the eye and said, "I love you...so much."

It's impossible to overstate the impact of euphoria, relief and exhaustion that combine in such a moment, but it was felt by every one of us present.

Charlie has returned to our world. The prayers, good wishes and kind thoughts are combining with Charlie's incredible fighting strength to produce an outcome that we simply had not expected so soon.

We know there is still a long road ahead of us, but the ability to communicate so meaningfully so soon after his accident, and on his sister's birthday, has created a very special Remembrance Day for which we will always be grateful.

Thank you XX

It's difficult to add further words to this day. Like any brother and sister, they have their good days when they are really there for each other, and they have those days when you breathe a sigh of relief that they haven't actually killed each other. We'd been reminding him about his sister's birthday for a couple of days beforehand and I'd desperately hoped he might be able to say some sort of birthday greeting. His voice was high pitched and very hoarse – the tube in his throat had impacted on his vocal chords. We'd expected to have to prompt him more – but the speech just came out.

In line with the 'one parent at a time' rule, I'd had to leave the ward whilst one of the doctors examined him. I knew nothing of what was happening and was sat in the waiting room oblivious to the scene that was unfolding nearby, but one of the nurses opened the door, clearly brimming with emotion and said, "I don't want to say too much, but you might want to go back in the ward. It's okay for both parents to be there right now."

As I knelt down beside him, his mother asked him if he wanted to say anything to me. And then, after 11 days of silence, his first slow, hesitant sentence to me, "I love you...so much." I couldn't speak. Tears flowed. There was no holding back in such a moment. His five words were an affirmation that those endless hours spent by his side had played their part, they'd had an impact, they'd reached him. So many times, I'd wondered how much he was hearing, how much, if anything, was getting through to his locked in world.

If there's one piece of solid advice I'd give to anybody in a similar situation, it's keep talking. It doesn't matter how many times you repeat yourself, just believe that every word makes a difference. I'd even taken his GCSE text books to read them to him in the hope that some of that knowledge might stay with him, helping support him after so many lost weeks in school. I'd love to say that it made a difference, but I have to be honest! I got bored of it very quickly and went on the chat about current affairs and what was happening with everybody at home instead.

The rush of emotion and adrenaline on that day had an inevitable result by the evening. I relaxed and was utterly exhausted. The noise of the ward swiftly faded as I lay on the camp bed and I sank into a deep and, at last, restful sleep. That most wonderful element in life of meaningful communication was well on its way to a full return and whatever else Charlie may still have to go through, I'd know clearly what he felt every step of the way.

Charlie's Journey - 13/11

Apologies for the lack of update yesterday. So many of you have asked where it was and if everything is okay, but, quite simply, exhaustion got the better of me and the words simply would not flow. And his journey is exhausting! But not just for us, particularly for Charlie.

Each day involves a steady stream of medical staff, all exceptional people. But I guess that after a while being woken in order to have somebody shine a light in your eye and squeeze your hand must become tiresome. And Charlie is as yet, of course, unable to perform tasks for himself, so the sheer effort required to fire the neurons from his injured brain and shoot them down to his hand on command is exhausting. And his speech is still slow.

But we're also seeing more of his humour! Today he started by insisting his name was George Michael! This was followed by an assertion that his middle name was Vindaloo. He's been telling the nurses about wanting Kentucky Fried Chicken. And when his mum asked if she could tell him a joke, he said, "Yes, but make it funny!"

He's chosen which films he's wanted to watch. He's reading the nurse's names off their badges when talking to them. And he's melted their hearts, firstly because he has beautiful eyes and secondly because when they've been helping him, he's told them they're kind.

Of course, we have no clear idea yet of any medium or long-term damage. But what hasn't been lost is the good-humoured lad wIth a cheeky sense of humour and an absolute heart of gold (and beautiful eyes)

Every day we are thankful. XX

We were told that sometimes during the first few days after waking from a coma, people with brain damage can come out with all sorts of unexpected words and phrases.

Charlie was no exception, which proved to be amusing at times and excruciatingly embarrassing at others. For some inexplicable reason, Charlie kept saying the 'n' word. This was made all the worse by the fact that a sizeable number of his nurses were people of colour. Sometimes, in still and quiet moments on the ward, a nurse would pass by and the stillness would be shattered by a resounding 'n' word emanating from Charlie's lips. No amount of coughing or pretending he hadn't said it could change the face-slapping embarrassment that followed such moments, and what almost made it worse was the kindness and understanding that he was met with. On one occasion, one lovely night nurse calmly wandered across and whispered in his ear, "Now Charlie. We don't use that word. Abi will get upset.". No anger, no frustration, no offence, just total kindness, gentleness and understanding, with a tangible connection through the meeting of eyes between nurse and her patient. It's impossible to overstate the deep admiration I have for those who cared for Charlie through the early days of recovery.

Charlie's Journey - 15/11

Sometimes, when your children won't go to sleep at night it's really irritating. Last night, Charlie bucked that trend. It was already difficult to think of settling as a teenage girl in the next cubicle was giving gratuitously offensive grief to her mother and the staff.

But then, at 1:15 am, Charlie piped up in his still slow and laboured speech, "Please may I go to the bathroom?"

And, with just a bit of help, he got up - stood up! Took a few steps. Sat up straight. Rarely in life have I felt so awake at that time in the morning. But there he was, just a fortnight after his life hung in the balance, standing. And several times during the day, he's done it again.

We've had a number of visits from staff who were with him when he first came in and during those first few days who are as astonished as we are at both the speed and consistency of his recovery so far. And whilst we don't want to become over optimistic, we can't help but feel a sense of hope that Christmas won't be spent up here.

And as always with Charlie, there are the moments where he melts everybody's hearts. He softly told a nurse she was a kind lady. He gently looked at me and said 'thank you'. He looked sad and said 'sorry'. But Charlie has nothing to be sorry for, because he's showing a strength of character that is even taking the seasoned staff caring for him by surprise.

And tonight, once again, as I settle down on the camp bed beside his, we will end our day with the same words we do every night at home.

"Love you, Son."

"Love you, Dad."

I take so many things for granted. One is the ability to go to the bathroom unaided when I need to, something that was only briefly interrupted following surgery a few years ago. In Charlie's case, he's always been a particularly private lad, so I worried desperately how he'd cope with the indignity of lavatorial needs. For several days, I'd helped in cleaning him when required. It's something that is uncontrollable and there were many incidents where everything needed to be changed just a few minutes after new sheets and clothes had been placed on him and on his bed. He'd become horribly sore at one point before becoming fully conscious, and each time he needed changing it gave me yet another insight into the extraordinary level of care and patience nursing staff show on a daily basis. Not once did any of them give the slightest indication of frustration. Not once did anybody express anything negative towards him. Quite the reverse. Each time the situation was dealt with to the accompaniment of 'it doesn't matter' style phrases, all of which were aimed solely at making sure Charlie felt okay. They succeeded. Not once has Charlie expressed any distress at the very personal indignity he faced. Not once did he seem upset. Indeed, he conveyed only gratitude throughout. It's difficult to think of many sectors in life where such a consistency of care and kindness is shown – all the more remarkable when you watch the staff working tirelessly through 12-hour shifts, all with face masks and PPE, no matter whether it was day or night, at the beginning of a shift or at the end.

Charlie's Journey - 18/11

As parents, we all treasure those days when our children make us proud. This strange world in which we find ourselves has at times brought us to the depths of despair through the sheer awfulness of what happened. But it has also been an exquisitely beautiful time where our hearts have heaved to bursting with the pride we feel as Charlie relentlessly battles his way to recovery.

In summary, he's now eating proper food, much to the relief of staff and family alike; his swift, slight of hand to remove his feeding tube several times each day proved an enormous challenge. He is now able to sit up without assistance and to stand and walk a little with aid. He is able to drink cups of tea - this is a tremendously important part of Charlie's diet! He is also, as some of you will now know, able to use his phone!!! Making contact with his friends is giving him a huge boost, although he is somewhat over optimistic about his recovery time. To all those he's told about coming home next week, I'm afraid it's not going to happen that soon.

Charlie still has a significant level of immobility down his left side and his right eye is struggling with focus. They're still looking at him as a suitable candidate for the 3-month intensive rehabilitation programme, which will be eight hours of hard slog every day.

Nonetheless, we continue to be astonished at Charlie's progress in just 18 days. And each evening as I head back to the hospital to be by his side until early afternoon the next day, he phones me several times to check on the progress of my journey to know for sure what time I'll be there. Everything we do for him is met with a warm, loving gratitude. And every hour of every day is filled with a relentless sense of pride.

As always, thank you so much for your kindness, love, prayers and good wishes. We are feeling the impact every day.

The feeding tube! Oh my goodness, how Charlie hated that! It must be horribly uncomfortable! There were several other habits that he had to learn to control or cope with. One was picking at the scabs around his head, both from the impact wounds and from the brain pressure probe on the top. The other was an extraordinary ability to remove his feeding tube within a matter of a very few seconds even as we sat beside him. Sadly, it was almost immediately followed by the process of re insertion which made the poor lad gag every single time. The wonderful sight of him taking his first few sips of tea was met with the same response and delight as when you first see your toddler perform a similar task independently. I felt the same pride that I'd felt when he was little, but this time there was relief in equal measure.

One surprise, as well as a sign of the times, was his ability to start using his phone to communicate with his friends. He was unable to use his left hand, but the quickest adaption of all was his ability to message one-handed and ignore his left hand completely. His newly reinstated ability to communicate with his friends did, however, reveal a significant lack of understanding about how seriously he'd been hurt and just how long his recovery could take.

The reality of timescale and physical capability is one element that is still a struggle several months on. Charlie underestimated how swiftly he would recover; he continues four months on to overestimate what he should be doing and the level to which he has healed. Conversations about staying safe occur every single day. Reminders of how any bump to the wrong part of his head could result in further temporary or permanent damage at this stage are necessary, but largely ignored. This was brought sharply in to focus when he went through a few days of falling down the stairs, thankfully mostly just the last few, as he became over-confident. One fall resulted in a bang on the back of his head followed almost immediately by temporary paralysis on his left side and a late evening trip to A&E.

Another side effect is a weakened ability to feel his own body temperature. When a 'Beast from the East' weather front arrived, Charlie spent time outside unaware of how cold he was getting. He thought this was great – how cool not to feel too cold. However, the risk of becoming too cold was all too evident on his return home, when he realised just how low his temperature had become and he required a slow, careful heat up.

Charlie's Journey - 21/11

Three weeks! Time and reality seem abstract concepts. Yet the days have formed into some sort of routine around travelling up each evening, making sure Charlie is relaxed and settled and then engaging with the many visits mainly during the mornings before catching the train home with another few items to wash.

For Charlie, time and reality are even harder to grasp. As his brain slowly begins its healing process, it's clear how much he is endeavouring to place everything in the right order and relate his life to each hospital day. The toughest bit for a lad who likes to be out and active so much is the sheer amount of time he has to spend in bed.

But his physical recovery continues to astonish all who have worked with him. He is now able to walk a fair distance, to dress himself and even double knot his shoe laces. And he's regularly asking to stand up and to go for a walk. Today he had his first trip outside the hospital in his wheelchair, leading to a Little Britain moment. I wheeled him up the road across the bumps and up an incline so that he could see Ruskin Park. He'd said that's where he wanted to go - I should have asked, "Are you sure?", for as we pulled into the gateway with me a little out of breath, he looked straight ahead and said, "I wanna go back to the ward".

And in the last couple of days, we have laughed. Today I even got a laugh out loud from him. He's very much seeing the funny side of things and engaging in a great deal of mischievous humour along the way.

Today we also got a glimpse of how much people who meet him grow to like him. Two of the nurses that had looked after him in HDU took time out of their lunch break to come up to the ward, say hello and see how he is. And one has said that next time he goes up to Ruskin Park, she'll see if they'll let her out to join him. Even in the midst of injury, with so much of him still hidden, his ability to engage with others seems undiminished.

These days at the end of November proved to be the most heartening and encouraging. There we times when Charlie said that he felt no emotion and, in particular, that he felt no anger. Nobody could. He was delightful. He wanted to keep doing things, albeit for short bursts, and his interaction with everybody was entirely positive. It seemed like he really appreciated being alive and most definitely appreciated the adults around him and the care they were giving. He wasn't awkward or demanding. Even when he was tired, he'd still make the effort to follow instructions. He made sure to make eye contact when reminded. He was polite. It was like the accident had washed away any personality flaw he might have had before and we'd just been left with the beautiful parts. They say personalities often change after a brain injury and it just seemed at this point Charlie's changes were utterly positive.

Charlie's charm also shone through. This made a difference through the journey of hospital rehabilitation. Make no mistake, everybody on the team gives 100% to every patient, but there was a clear sense that they all really enjoyed the time they spent with

Charlie and the emotional engagement was tangible. It's the chemistry that can change the whole process, transforming the mundane and repetitive activities into banter-fuelled enjoyment. Charlie still refers to his 'friends' at King's, a friendship that enabled them to break through the barriers of a very self-conscious teenage boy in treatment that very often required close and intimate physical contact. There were many occasions when I marvelled at just what he'd let them do, even when I could see he still felt awkward, but their compassion, kindness and professionalism broke straight through every aspect of his awkwardness. There simply aren't enough superlatives in the English language to adequately describe my respect and gratitude for every single one of them.

Charlie's Journey - 23/11

Our gratitude for your prayers, positive thoughts and kindness remains undiminished as we get new insights into the extraordinary rate of recovery thus far.

We had the results through from Charlie's MRI, which show multiple damage to exons across several different areas of his brain. The consultant said that on a rising risk scale of 1 - 3, on admission Charlie was on 3 - that caused a shockwave of hollowness in my stomach as he spoke, from which the emotion is still overwhelming several hours later. But the current rate of Charlie's progress has astonished everybody, including those so familiar with head trauma. At this stage, of course, it's still really early to know the extent of any long-term damage. But so far, we have witnessed somewhat of a miracle.

We're committing ourselves to the intensive rehabilitation programme. This usually lasts for 3 - 6 months, but we see the commitment as an investment in Charlie at a moment in his life when he absolutely needs it. With

Charlie's rate of progress so far, the consultant actually believes the time required could be far less. Home for Christmas really is a possibility.

We are so acutely aware of our story being positive where others are not so fortunate. In the bed next to ours lay a young child with a brain tumour where the prognosis is nowhere near as optimistic. And the other day I chatted to a parent whose child had received an organ for transplant - one life lost and another saved. Each day from Charlie's bed we see the air ambulance landing and feel the pain of all those affected by the events around its arrival. If the walls could talk, the range of emotions and experience they would speak of would be extraordinary.

So our gratitude lacks adequate superlatives, as does our pride in our extraordinary son.

Thank you XX

It seems incredible now that at this stage we were looking at the possibility of Charlie being up there for a full six months. So many thoughts overwhelmed me. How on earth would I cope with the financial requirements without working? How would I cope with the practicalities? Home was a two-hour journey, with three dogs and an 89-year-old mother who also needed a level of care and who was prevented from leaving the house due to Covid-19 restrictions. At various points in the day, it would become overwhelming. The deep trauma of what had happened to Charlie was still raw, and the anxieties of keeping afloat in real life piled on top of an already heavy emotional burden.

Thankfully, there's a whole team of incredible people who are based within the hospital to give guidance and support to parents as well as to the patient. Several months on that support is as strong as ever and whilst there's an inevitability that most of the graft is down to me as a parent, it makes a real difference to know that I can at least pick up the phone or ping an email when it all gets too much.

Charlie's Journey - 29/11

What a joyful experience for Charlie to spend a couple of nights in his own bed after a month in hospital. It was a joy for me, too 🍎 .

Heading home to familiar surroundings also brought a sense of reality. Charlie expected a little too much of himself initially and after falling within an hour of being home, we nearly ended up with a trip to A&E! Thankfully we felt he'd be okay and as the 48 hours progressed so did Charlie.

The dogs went loopy! They've also had a month where they've not had the regular human contact and they've really missed Charlie.

Whilst we've been relaxing, others have been pulling off amazing feats on Charlie's behalf, raising funds to support us all through this challenge and also for the life-saving Air Ambulance, without which our story may have had a tragic end. Thank you to Weald Triathlon for their epic efforts throughout the weekend, still going strong as I write. And likewise to the daughter and father who jogged and walked an amazing 26 miles round Bewl Reservoir yesterday. The continued kindness and support is extraordinary. And it makes a huge difference both psychologically and practically. We're able to be up here to support Charlie - a key factor in him receiving a place on the Intensive Rehabilitation Programme.

Tomorrow that's what Charlie will start. This morning he was worried about coming back, but the weekend at home has also reminded him why it's necessary. And, yet again, he's showing the determination that's needed to succeed. The staff up here at King's all believe in him. The lead consultant has formed a really good bond with him and has been particularly struck by Charlie's processing of the whole experience. And you - every single one of you that is rooting for him - you're all making a difference. You're changing what could so easily become a draining experience into an adventure.

So whilst my sign-off today lacks originality, it's as heartfelt as it has been every single day through this extraordinary experience...

Thank you XX

It was the most extraordinary feeling to be able to walk out of the hospital with Charlie's suitcase for our first weekend leave. The journey home was arduous, and we had to stop a couple of times when Charlie felt nauseous, but it was also such an incredible relief. All he'd been through, and here he was just one month after I thought I'd lost him, actually sitting beside me in the car on his way home for the weekend.

It was also a reminder to him that he wasn't fully healed. He'd tried to change his trousers just a few minutes after our arrival, and being in the familiar setting of home, he'd done what he always does: he stood up and lifted his leg. The weakness in his balance instantly caused him to fall, resulting in a large bang on his arm, another bump on the head and several hours of anxiety at the possibility of further damage. Thankfully the blow to the head didn't result in any side effects and the injured arm was treated back in the hospital the following week. It did, though, serve to remind him that even though he had been allowed back home, he wasn't as recovered as he believed himself to be.

Charlie's Journey - 04/12

[This blog included a photograph of the Air Ambulance landing on the roof of the hospital. We had a clear and direct view of the landing zone from Charlie's bed]

This is the sight that serves as a daily reminder of the response that saved Charlie's life. It brings back every emotion, but primarily there's an extraordinary sense of relief, gratitude and astonishment at just how far Charlie has come in the 5 weeks he's been here.

And it's just 5 weeks!

This week, he's had daily sessions focused on his physical and neurological rehabilitation. He's attending Hospital School, which he started two days earlier than planned at his request. His Mum also took him up high street where he did some Christmas shopping and wrapped up the presents afterwards. His voice is almost completely normal, although his speech is still a little slow at times with limited intonation.

And he's currently obsessed with playing Guess Who, an obsession that will soon require the administration of sedatives for those of us playing with him 😫*.*

So, after another successful week with continued progress, we'll be hitting the road hopefully early this afternoon for his second weekend of home leave.

Once again, I'm afraid it's strict shielding for Charlie. I know he's suggested to some that he could meet up, but the conditions of home leave at weekends are very tight.

And, as always, a heartfelt thank you to you all for keeping us in your prayers, thoughts and love XX

Hmmm! I'd really hoped that with the fall and realisation of a long journey still to travel, Charlie might be wishing to show caution. Not at all! Apparently, it's a common trait in those recovering from a brain injury that the consequence button all but disappears. Charlie's narrative was that he was pretty indestructible! If a Jeep couldn't finish him off, then meeting up with his friends and risking catching Coronavirus certainly weren't going to do him harm.

In practical terms, it meant that leaving him alone just wasn't an option. The minute he sensed an opportunity, he would attempt to head off outside, insisting that he was perfectly okay and that no harm would come to him. It made daily tasks such as heading for the supermarket high risk activities, all undertaken in a desperate rush before racing back to make sure he hadn't disappeared off.

Charlie's Journey - 7/12

So, the miracle lad continues to confound the experts! Today the psychologist chatted with him at length, genuinely fascinated by his thought process as he tries to piece together what happened on that night. We still don't actually know exactly what happened and hope that in the fulness of time we'll get the complete picture. In the course of the conversation, she mentioned that she'd seen early reports talking of multiple fractures in his face, shoulders and pelvis only to see a later report that referred to the absence of fractures!

A little later in the day, one of the neurology team was explaining the damage to the brain. Alongside the statement that the brain doesn't regenerate the damaged cells, he also said that Charlie simply does not present as the MRI scans suggest he should. He shouldn't be able to do as much as he is.

I still believe in miracles ⋏⋏⋏⋏⋏.

And with each passing day, I realise just how much I love the lad. He practises running. It looks awkward and a little uncoordinated, but I well up with emotion and want to hug him tightly because I see that determination in him to be completely as he was before. At the weekend he rode his bike round the garden. He practises jumping just like he did when he was little, to develop his physical capability. As I write and hold the images in my mind, the tears flow. I'm so proud of this beautiful lad, so desperately willing him on to heal perfectly, so grateful at the extraordinary healing so far and still resolutely determined to walk alongside him on this journey, no matter what the sacrifice may be.

The words that I shouted in such pain and despair at the scene I now say with complete and utter pride: "That's my son!"

It's really good to re-read this! As I'm adding my narrative, I've got a clear picture in my head of the exact moment I watched his early attempts at running up the corridor in the hospital. There was a beautiful innocence about it, in just the same way as he used to practice new physical skills when he was a toddler. On those days, when it seems insurmountably difficult, holding those images in my head takes me back to that place of hope, of pride, of love.

Charlie's Journey - 13/12

It's not usual for a trip to Tesco to feel like it's something special, but context is everything!

Our two-hour drive home on Friday afternoon was almost entirely Charlie's exploration of everything that happened from the moment of the accident through to his full awakening from the coma. Charlie isn't just working out the event of the injury, but is now piecing together the story of his recovery so far. He wanted to fill in the gaps from the bits he remembers when it felt like it was a dream; the part of the story from before he was moving and speaking for himself, where every movement was so carefully choreographed by the team. Sitting him up, holding him securely, protecting him. It's just four weeks since we were delighting in the success of his eyes moving in the right direction and the ability to give a squeeze with just his right hand. And that special moment when he leant forward into my shoulder for a hug, unable to speak or return the hug, but clearly showing an expression of pleasure in the warmth of the contact between father and son.

The questions that were most surprising were the ones where he asked how it felt for those of us watching and supporting his recovery. The sense of empathy emanating from his questions were not only poignant, but they showed a really encouraging aspect of his neurological recovery - he's still got feelings and is able to express some of them.

And then came Tesco. Something that is usually little more than a task of necessity was the top of his list for activity as we arrived back at Gills Green. So during the evening, we popped up there. I wasn't sure what he'd feel, whether revisiting the site of the accident would cause trauma, would trigger a memory, would raise anxiety. It didn't feel like that at all! We had the privilege of meeting two of the three Tesco staff that were first responders on the scene that night, both of whom were simply delighted to see him; three people whose training kicked in at the most perilous of moments in Charlie's life and made the difference very probably between life and death. All round the store we met staff who greeted him with delight, who knew his story and who exuded a genuine warmth on seeing him. That short experience was yet another reminder of the care, love and support that continues to make such a difference through this most challenging of journeys. It was another reminder to us that the scales balance - for all the awfulness that came with the accident itself, the extraordinary humanity shown continues to exemplify the very best in our community. The short shopping trip with those brief greetings gave an entirely new meaning to the phrase, 'every little helps'!

Later today It's back to the hard work. Charlie's so frustrated at the return to hospital, but we have the knowledge that due to his remarkable and sustained recovery so far, it looks like we're going to be allowed to have a full fortnight at home over the Christmas and New Year. It really is so much more than we dared hope for and it gives Charlie a real sense of purpose during the coming week.

Since leaving hospital, Charlie has often said that he doesn't experience emotion. That's really hard to hear, but I also believe it's not totally accurate. When he's said or done things that cause negative emotions in me, I've told him about the impact. His initial response has usually been along the lines of him having no filter or emotion, but he has then attempted to moderate his behaviours and the things he says. I can see times when he starts to say something that might offend, but then holds himself back, so the empathy button is still working. He still cares. Whilst he can't currently express it well, he still loves. The important relationships in his life still matter. It's so important, even though it's difficult, not to lose heart and to keep believing that this part of him will return fully.

Charlie's Journey – 21.12.20

Tier 4 lockdown beat me to the shops...
It's peeing with rain...
I still haven't managed to finish the housework...
I haven't managed to get the Christmas lights on the front of the house...
But I've never been more aware of how fortunate I am this Christmas!

Charlie's Journey – 25.12.20

Rarely in life has my gratitude on this day provoked such a depth of emotion. So I hope you'll accept my heartfelt thanks for your love, prayers, care and support through what I simply could never have imagined.
Merry Christmas to you all XXX
And I've just opened my Christmas card from Charlie, in which his first sentence, written so painfully slowly, says 'thank you for staying with me in hospital' 😊

The contrast between the lack of preparedness in the house and my emotional state couldn't have been greater. The initial prognosis had made Charlie's return home seem such a long way off, yet there we were celebrating Christmas with him at home. With all the frantic back and forth between home and the hospital, Christmas just didn't register on my conscious thoughts. Having planned to do a big shopping trip the Monday after his return home, the announcement was made of a sudden lockdown. But Christmas was far from cancelled. Special days usually provoke reflection. Christmas was always a big event when the children were little, with the tree so carefully decorated and presents arranged perfectly under it. For some years, Christmas dinner involved at least a dozen people sitting round the table, with noise and laughter. Divorce brought an inevitable constraint on the day and Charlie's accident simply became the main focus of all endeavour. Yet, I genuinely can't remember ever feeling such gratitude as I did on that day and the words he'd written in the card were profoundly moving. I knew I'd made a difference.

Charlie's Journey - 12.01.21

It's a while since I posted and a number of people have asked how Charlie is getting on.

The great bit is that Charlie's physical recovery seems to be holding well. He still has some difficulty with his left side, which can cease to fully function without warning, but he's managing incredibly well.

Neurologically, the journey to recovery is much longer. The knowledge that damaged brain cells do not regenerate still haunts me and causes overwhelming emotion at unexpected moments.

Charlie expresses his own feelings of how he wished the accident hadn't happened, which sometimes take him to dark places in his thoughts. And, as is so often the case following brain injury, some of his behaviours present in line with neuro-diverse conditions such as ADHD and ASD. We get stuck on particular loops of thought that can be frustrating and exhausting to break through.

To add to the challenge, with London hospitals now packed with Covid cases, Charlie's rehabilitation can no longer continue at King's. It's a real blow and we're in the process of looking at how best to access more local therapies whilst remaining under the oversight of King's. In spite of being so keen to get home for Christmas, Charlie has been keen to get back to continue and complete his therapy.

From a parent's perspective, this bit of the journey is proving every bit as tough, albeit in a different way, as what has gone before - and every bit as emotional. When I catch sight of the small patch on the back of his head where the hair hasn't yet regrown, it provokes the deepest, most painful emotions - my child is still broken and fixing him is a rocky, uphill, challenging road.

When you're in the midst of a traumatic event, you can barely turn around for people that are there for you and wanting to help. Those people are still there, of course, but life moves on for everybody and it's inevitable that we all just have to get on with what we need to do. This is the long haul. It's unrealistic to expect others to have the capacity to be able to support as so much of the effort in rehabilitation coming through the conversation between parent and child. There are days where almost every interaction is in some way a deep, challenging process of rehabilitation. Every sentence has to be thought about, every response diagnosed for inner meaning. Those are days when it's exhausting.

Some interactions take place at odd hours. Charlie went through a phase of coming into my room very late at night or in the early hours with questions about when his hair might regrow over the small bald patch, when his eye might start to fully focus.

However, every day it serves as a reminder that I'm his dad, that he needs me and that no matter what time of the day or night it is, he can come to me because I'm his constant.

5 - Guilt

There are many aspects to feelings of guilt when your child suffers as Charlie has done. The first and most obvious is connected inextricably with not being there when the accident happened. I've relived every conversation of the day, where Charlie had wanted to do something with me for Halloween and then changed his mind. My final call to him before the accident was where I told him I'd eat my meal then return home and we'd do something together. I'd hung around in the village a few miles away because my daughter had wanted to stay there with her old school friends – but what if I'd just insisted he'd spent the evening with me instead of going out with his mates. Yet at 14 years old they can't, and shouldn't, be spending all their time with their parents. And, of course, in Charlie's case, the activity surrounding the accident wasn't high risk, wasn't adventurous, wasn't remotely rebellious; it was crossing the road.

Latterly, the reasons for guilt changed. One of the inevitable common reactions with brain trauma is anger. Charlie has expressed this on so many occasions. The journey home from the hospital for Christmas should have been one of unadulterated joy and celebration, but for the entire journey Charlie was berating everybody and everything. The Jeep driver, drivers in general, me for not berating the Jeep driver, the Government for likely Covid-19 lockdown restrictions, and different groups within society for whom he had no actual hatred; there was simply an overload of pent-up anger. None of that caused guilt in me. It was all what I'd been told to expect.

What caused the guilt were some of the feelings I experienced. I'd been so looking forward to Charlie coming home, it was just the best Christmas present ever. But on that two-and-a-half-hour journey, there were moments when I wanted to turn the car round and take him back to the hospital, where I had a sense of frustration that he was responsible for spoiling his moment, where I felt it was unfair that he was tarnishing the moment that should have been so special...where I was angry with him! Yet how could I possibly feel any anger? I'd felt a more intense pain than anything else I'd experienced in life on the night of his accident, yet here I was feeling frustration and anger at some of the things he was saying.

And I wanted to tell him forcefully about how much it had hurt when he'd been hit, tell him of the utter torment I'd been through, tell him how on every single day I'd wept at his suffering and his pain. How dare he not share the same sense of joy and relief at coming home that I'd felt earlier that day!

Charlie had wanted to come home. Yet by the following day, he wanted to go back to hospital, to complete his rehabilitation and then to be, in his view, back to normal. And at that point I felt hurt. Yes, with the chaos of the journeys back and forth to London, I'd not managed to get the house decorated in time for Christmas and there wasn't yet a tree. And yes, the house was a bit of a mess because as a single parent I had no domestic back-up for such tasks. And yes, lockdown restrictions had been announced on the day after I collected him meaning I wouldn't be able to get to the shops for all those last-minute bits and pieces that had formed such a big part of Christmases when the children were little. But after just 24 hours, at a time when I'd been so delighted to have him home, how could he want to go back? How could he not want to be at home with his family? How could he be so ungrateful? And why was he being so awkward and argumentative about wanting to go out with his mates when he knew he couldn't? All he seemed to want to do was argue and antagonise and, once again, I felt frustration and anger, which occasionally I expressed followed by a huge feeling of guilt for feeling any such emotion! I should just be grateful, happy, relieved, in the mood for total celebration!

There's also an underlying guilt that I experienced within the hospital setting.

Charlie's recovery was progressing at an astonishing rate, but it clearly wasn't the same experience for some others. I had several conversations when asked by fellow parents about how Charlie was getting on and I was wholly optimistic. But when I asked about their children, there were those for who the prognosis was not so encouraging and a few for whom the journey was going to end all too soon. I also chatted one day with a lady whose child had received a heart transplant. She was battling with a whole mixture of emotions, because after the long wait for a suitable donor heart, she knew that it had only been possible through the death of another. The stark awareness that your joy comes at the expense of others is difficult to comprehend when you're not in that position, but I understood just a little from my own feelings for those parents facing such desperate times.

6 - Where's My Son?

Anger is possibly the hardest thing to deal with. When Charlie first came out of the coma, his heart was beautiful. He expressed only kind thoughts and gratitude. And he said on several occasions that he no longer had any angry feelings inside, feelings that had caused problems on so many occasions before the accident.

I felt encouraged, uplifted, hopeful! Could the accident have caused a positive personality change, and removed the difficult bits of Charlie's personality that had so often provoked a negative fallout in the past?

It didn't last!

The anger grew inside, seeping out bit by bit through negative comments about all sorts of random things in the two weeks preceding his departure from hospital. By the time Christmas was over, the anger was beginning to fill sizeable chunks of every day. He resented having his 'freedom taken away', a situation not only caused by his brain injury, but exacerbated by the Covid-19 lockdown that began in our part of the country the weekend we arrived home.

One of the repetitive comments that surfaced through many conversations was, "Perhaps I should have been killed, then I wouldn't have to do this!", which then accompanied any task he didn't fancy doing along with, "I'm the one that had the brain injury!" to justify any lack of effort at any given point. The latter comment was fairly easy to dismiss; the former provoked dismay and distress. Each time he said it, I reminded him of how many people loved him deeply, how many rooted for him through those darkest days and how we'd have all been utterly devastated had his accident been fatal. It should be more straightforward to rationalise such comments as merely an expression of frustration on his part that he wasn't 'normal', that he wasn't like he was before. But in the midst of heated conversations, battling through his intransigence, it still sent a shudder down my spine. Alongside that rides the concern as to whether or not this anger will last; will he still be this angry in 10 years' time? What impact is that likely to have on relationships and his employment potential? When you read of situations where personalities change through a brain injury, it's rarely positive and some of his anger was directed at specific individuals, such as the driver. In those angry moments, he expressed a desire for physical retribution. How would that play out? Would he end up getting into a physical altercation at some point further down the line? What would happen if his anger spilled when out and about and he got into a fight? One small punch to his head in the wrong position could easily render him disabled. Yet, he refused to acknowledge any possibility of danger.

Likewise, Charlie's anger manifested itself through intolerance. He expressed views of outright hatred towards different groups and anger towards those who sought to balance those views. Any challenge to his viewpoint was met with "I don't care! I hate them!". This was particularly hard to deal with as Charlie hadn't been filled with hate before the accident. Yes, he'd set about winding up his sister at every mealtime when she was vegan, but it had never made him angry before. Now he was expressing his views with spite and venom, views that none of us hold and all of us abhor, and it's really difficult to just try and palm it off under the guise of "It's just his brain injury talking".

This is the bit I've found the toughest. Like so many other relatives of those with a brain injury, you see changes in the one you love. We all want the fairy-tale ending, but reality comes along and reshapes how things pan out. In Charlie's case, he has repeatedly said he doesn't feel emotion. What that actually means, is that he can say incredibly hurtful things and not respond to the impact it has on others. With that lack of emotion comes a palpable sense of bereavement for those around him. It's the same body and many of the same habits, but as I've said so often when asked how he's doing, there are things that are missing. Right now, it's difficult to know for sure how much is simply down to being a teenager, how much is down to the injury and how much will return. Whilst I'm grateful every day that he's here, there are also plenty of moments that are distressing, exhausting and that leave me saddened for the bits of my son that I've lost.

Whilst most of Charlie remains intact, there are differences are clear to see. A common feature is that the patient presents characteristics of autistic spectrum or ADHD. Likewise, brain injuries can often amplify existing traits of both. This can result in becoming stuck in a loop following a particular narrative, which creates their context for any given action or sentence you may use. It throws a wide ball into the simplest of interactions and I've found it both distressing and confusing on so many occasions. Simple statements from me are met with an accusation of motive that simply isn't there, causing conflict along the way. The result can all too easily become long silences and words unspoken for fear of starting yet another lengthy explanation, another sigh of despair. It's at those moments when no matter how well you are supported, no matter how many affirmations from others about the 'great job you're doing', you feel so desperately alone and downhearted. I'm tremendously fortunate in having such a supportive and understanding partner who relentlessly encourages me, but there are times when I have to admit with shameful honesty that I'm not doing a great job.

There are also challenges in how others see and respond to a child with a brain injury. Make no mistake, Charlie's school has been amazing with its support for his rehabilitation. There are, though, just the odd occasions when a response to his actions is based on a system that is designed for the neuro-typical child. When Charlie was in hospital, pupils in his school were brilliant, but there's always one! That particular one messaged on a gaming site one night saying it would have been better if Charlie had died in the accident. Charlie took offence and made a few threats to the individual concerned. The threats were totally unacceptable in their tone and in their language, threats that seemed completely out of character to my son – but they also reflect the frontal lobe injury that disinhibits communication. They did little more than to exemplify the lack of filter in his thought process. The threats wouldn't have resulted in anything and were little more than bravado and testosterone which fills the gaming and social media superhighway. Alas, the parents of the individual complained and the consequence was to place Charlie in a special unit with just three others whilst a Risk Assessment process was undertaken, a process that was due to last two weeks.

In searching for my pre-accident son, and in his own search for his pre-accident self, familiarity through routines and social interactions with his peers were essential features on his pathway to rehabilitation. Yet here I was, dropping him off, totally unprepared for what was actually happening, seeing the hollowness mist over his eyes. As I drove away from the unit, I was utterly crestfallen on his behalf. I was trying so hard to help him become comfortable with himself and I'd had to take him to what felt like an outpost for misfits. I didn't even make it to the car before the tears started to flow. He had been removed from his social setting, his friends, the routine of the school bus, from normality. The lad that I was so desperately trying to bring back fully was slipping away. I'd watched his entire body slump as I could see his belief that there were those in his school who saw him as mentally deficient. It contrasted so starkly with the fortnight preceding this, where he'd really started to show good, interactive humour. He'd made a real effort to be helpful, engaged, positive and take responsibility when things went wrong.

Charlie has spent a lifetime trying to fit in. He's relentlessly pushed to one side the labels assigned to him through his school life and just wanted to be 'normal'. Now he was overwhelmed with a sense that he was being punished for having a brain injury, and once more his mind became fogged with anger and resentment. Once more my son disappeared behind the red mist. Once more there was a hill to climb to rediscover him under the burden he felt.

There's no escaping the overwhelming feeling that I return to regularly. My son is broken and I'm struggling to fix it. I try to find the right words, the best approach, the most positive response, but time and again I feel like I've failed, let him down. I just simply got it wrong.

All of the above is tough. I don't have any great words of wisdom, terrific solutions of meaningful platitudes that cause others to rub their chin with an affirmative 'Hmmm'. My approach has been to regularly revisit the photographs that I took in the hospital, not only of the first hours and days when he was so poorly, but of the golden moments during his recovery. I find it helps never to lose sight of what we've been through and re-focus on the miracle that has taken place so far. Yes, there are bits of Charlie that aren't currently there. But we'll get through it. And most importantly, I make sure that no matter how tough the day is, there's still room for humour, because in the moment of a smile, eye to eye, the bond is once again strengthened, and the sting taken out of the wound.

Since he's come home though, there are also things that make me realise just how much of my son is still there. Hanging on a hook in the kitchen is a small sticky note. The handwriting is scratchy and difficult to read. It was written when he still had very limited mobility in his left hand. There aren't many words, but they're incredibly meaningful: "Thank you for staying with me in hospital". He wrote the same in his Christmas card to me, which still sits beside my bed.

The answer to the question is, of course, he's still there. Even when the old familiar bits of him seem well and truly hidden, there are enough flashes of him to encourage and uplift. I have to remind myself frequently that this isn't a quick journey, that his physical recovery happens at a very different speed to his neurological recovery. What I have to do is be his constant, his link with life before the accident, his guide when he gets it wrong, his celebrant when he's getting it right. And whatever else may be happening, the bond remains strong. He's still my son and he's still in there.

7 - Consultants

Let me start by saying that I have the greatest of admiration for consultants. Not only are they very clever, but their judgements are the crucial basis for the roadmap that guides us all through the journey of treatment and recovery.

However, they don't always cheer you up!

Several nurses told me that consultants do tend to give you the bleakest potential outcomes as well as assessing how well they're doing. Inevitably, the sense of what could go wrong causes deep anxiety and can leave you with an entire suitcase of worries. But it's also important to recognise that their knowledge provides you with a reality check. I was told directly that on a scale of 1 to 3, where 3 is the most dangerous, Charlie was on 3 upon his arrival at the hospital. Thankfully this information was only imparted once he was well on his journey of recovery. What it also did was affirm the sense of miracle in what we'd all seen.

On more than one occasion, I listened intently to many words, endeavoured to take in as much as possible (often having had little sleep) and smiled gratefully as they departed. The smile, of course, was designed merely to deflect from any sense of ignorance, exhaustion, or the fact that I'd probably got bits of hair sticking up from my inability to groom properly in the hospital toilet. What I did have to do very quickly after their visits was to write down those bits I could remember and understand in the hope that I'd be able to pass on information accurately.

I also have to be honest and say that my background of 33 years in education, which included significant time researching and leading training on learning processes, helped in shaping the very nature of the conversations I was able to have. I'm not on the same level by some margin, but I generally understood what was happening and my ability to hold my own as well as raise a few laughs was all helpful in supporting the positive relationships with the consultants.

Time and again, I had cause to marvel with extraordinary gratitude at the knowledge and care of the various consultants who worked with Charlie. Every single day, I was aware that he was receiving world class care from some of the finest medical minds. Whilst I may have felt some anxieties, I also had an enviable level of confidence with every element of his treatment every single day.

8 - Hope

Hope is difficult to quantify. It's an abstract concept. You can't buy a chunk of it. You can't train yourself to be filled with when things suddenly go wrong. But it's definitely something that I clung desperately to from the moment I arrived at the scene of the accident. And I find it's something that can be strengthened by others. It was whilst I was sitting in the waiting room that I first messaged out. I felt deeply alone in my own thoughts and anxieties and needed to call on the support of those who know me from the past and in the present. I sent out the first message, and within moments the messages started flowing in. The love, prayers and positive thoughts brought with them a sense of hope that the powers within the Universe would all work together to support Charlie and bring him through. Whatever beliefs any individual may hold, my belief is that it made a difference.

My sense of hope was also strengthened throughout the hospital days by hearing from those who had experienced similar situations, either personally or with a relative. Many of those messages came almost apologetically as people acknowledged that our situation wasn't about them, but they provided a source of hope in hearing the stories of recovery. It wasn't necessary to ask about specific injury details or find comparative recovery dates; it was enough just to know that the body is remarkable, that healing happens and that the human spirit is capable of surviving against tremendous odds.

Throughout my blogs, I know I created an overwhelming feeling of hope and positivity. None of that takes away from the fact that on some days it simply is all too much! There are still so many days when I feel utterly exhausted with it all, desperately wishing I could turn the clock back to before the accident. I look at Charlie's small bald patch and I'm overwhelmed with sadness for him because I know that he's self-conscious about it. I listen when he reacts in a way that wouldn't have happened before, or comes out with random sentences that seem to have been plucked from the sky and are heading nowhere, all with a sense of concern. I spend time trying to avoid particular flavours in food, such as garlic, and aromas in the kitchen, such as ketchup, as they trigger him. All of these things can inhibit the sense of hope of those early days.

That's where it's all important to remember. Right from the start I took photographs and filmed his early small steps of recovery. It's painful to remind myself of just how injured he was, but the images also show how far he's come in a relatively short time. And that's what gives hope for the future. Hope is very much needed during the challenging moments of the present and the future.

9 - Gratitude

Through all the paradoxical emotions and feelings during this whole experience, this is the one that remains at the very top of the list. No matter how hard it's been, or how hard it gets, every day when I look at Charlie, I'm grateful. Parenthood is rarely without a challenge, and there are many times through the years when I've felt that Charlie has brought more than his fair share. Perhaps this was the big opportunity for me to be able to put frustrations to one side and to relish the sheer joy of being a parent, to value every day knowing that it's a bonus, to ensure that whatever other messages I give my children they must know that they are loved.

Right from the first moments after the accident, I was filled with gratitude. For the friends who made sure they got hold of us to let us know. For the lady who was first to call for an ambulance. For the first responders from Tesco, who were there within moments of the impact. For the ambulance crew and police, all of whom have been in touch since, displaying the qualities that make them such outstanding people. For the Air Ambulance crew, who brought with them not only such expertise, but a real sense of reassurance at what was genuinely the most awful moment of my life.

Then there are all those extraordinary people we met at King's College Hospital. It's wrong to name any particular individuals, because no matter how little time they spent caring for Charlie and looking after us as relatives, they had an impact. Every single day they filled me with hope, encouragement, comfort, and Charlie still refers to them affectionately as friends. It's a measure of his gratitude and affection when he still relentlessly asks when we'll be able to visit them, to thank them and to have the opportunity to say goodbye after Covid restrictions denied it to us. I want to be able to see each and every one of them, to thank them and to hug them, but frankly they'd probably find me embarrassing. I like to think I'm good with words, but whatever phrases and sentences I might come out with, it simply wouldn't adequately express my heartfelt thanks for everything that they have done.

There were also so many people along the way, some of whom I've never met and some of whom still stop me in the street to ask if I'm Charlie's dad and how he's doing. There were those who shared their stories to bring encouragement, those who simply wrote a sentence of two for the same reason, those who reacted to the blogs with 'hearts' and 'likes', all of whom made a difference as I logged on each day. There were so many people who prayed, sent positive thoughts, practised healing. To this day I've no real explanation of how the multiple fractures simply disappeared, other than I believe all these people made a difference. There were people who baked cakes and made meals, who took Eleanor to the bus stop to get her to school, who shopped for my elderly mum who lives in an attached annexe, all while I was up at the hospital. There were those who contributed to the Just Giving page, who raised funds just to make it possible for us to get back and forth so that Charlie wasn't alone. As a result, Charlie's messages thanking me for staying at the hospital show the measure of how much it meant to him that he wasn't alone.

To every single one of you – thank you. You lifted us up when we were down, you shone light into a dark tunnel, you brought comfort when we felt discouraged. It made a difference. It brought so many positives to what would have been otherwise a traumatic experience. It changed the story for the better and it brought out the best of human kindness.

And I must also thank my Emily. Our relationship was in its infancy when the accident happened. There were endless times when I just had to leave, when plans were changed, when I just had to abandon her. Each time she showed understanding and acceptance. Each time her response was supportive.

I know that all of the above demonstrates just how fortunate I have been as a father living through such experience, and I know that there are fathers and parents out there who are not in the same position, who don't have such a supportive network or who don't feel they could share so publicly to look for support.

That's why, in moving forward, we've started Charlie Black CIC. I believe in creating a positive Karma, and if as a result of what we've been through, we can help others in their journey to recovery, then that's a fitting tribute to the courageous battle my son has fought. Thank you for your purchasing of this book in supporting what we do.

My final expression of gratitude has to be for my son, whose courage, determination and spirit has displayed qualities that are remarkable. He's taken all the support, both professional and personal, and has acted upon it to repay the efforts of those who gave it.

Thank you, Charlie. You've made it all worth it. Love you, Son.

Printed in Great Britain
by Amazon